Eight more piano duets in the five finger position for beginners and intermediate players

Beginner's parts can be played with both hands or just one

To inspire confidence in playing and reading music

and to be enjoyed

Published by Rosa Conrad
Copyright © Rosa Conrad 2013
All rights reserved

I
Plain Sailing

Intermediate

Calm, Lento

I
Plain Sailing

Beginner
Both hands two octaves higher

Calm, Lento

II
Shanty

Intermediate

II
Shanty

Beginner
Both hands one octave higher

III
Carousel

Intermediate

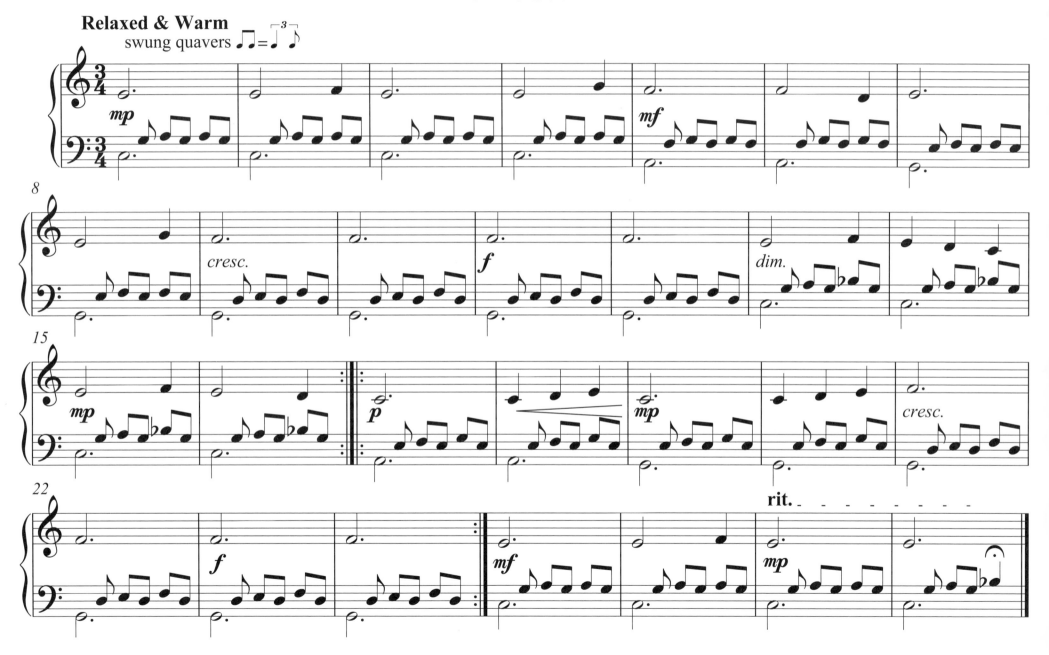

III
Carousel

Beginner
Both hands one octave higher

Relaxed & Warm

IV
Minor Waltz

Intermediate

IV
Minor Waltz

Beginner
Both hands two octaves higher

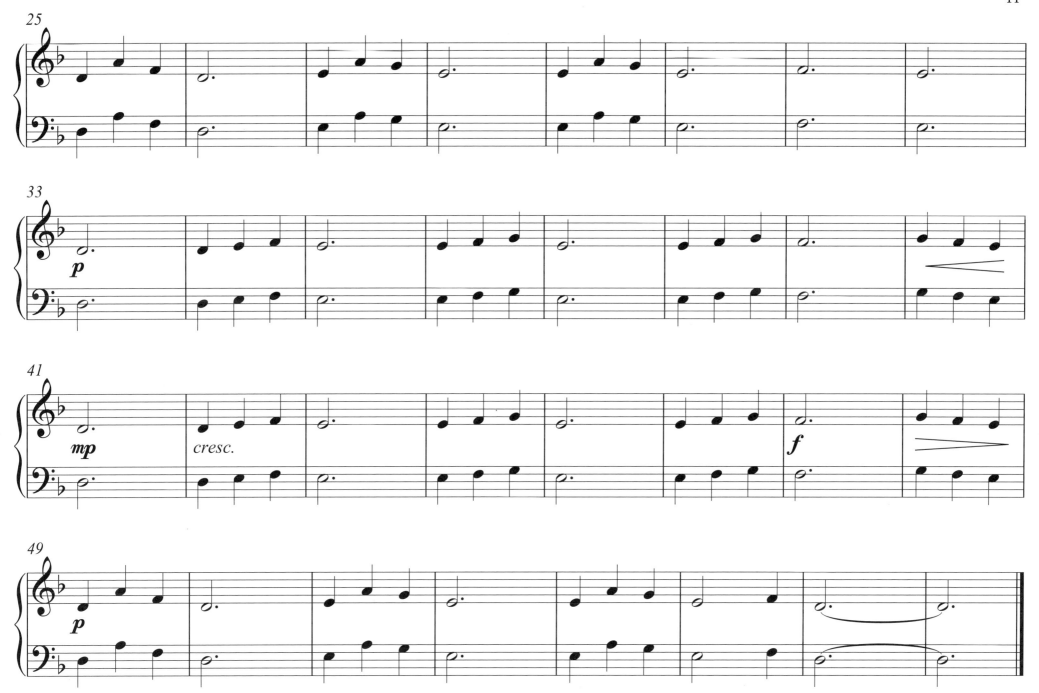

V
Keep Rolling

Intermediate

V
Keep Rolling

Beginner
Both hands two octaves higher

VI
Summer Journey

Intermediate

Andante

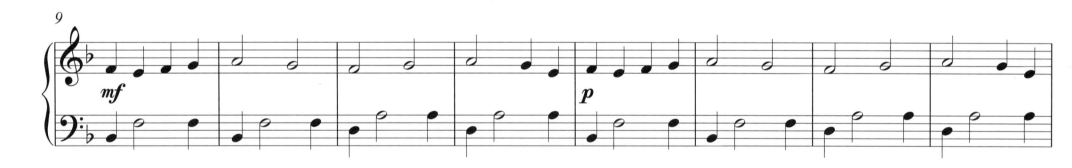

VI
Summer Journey

Beginner
Both hands two octaves higher

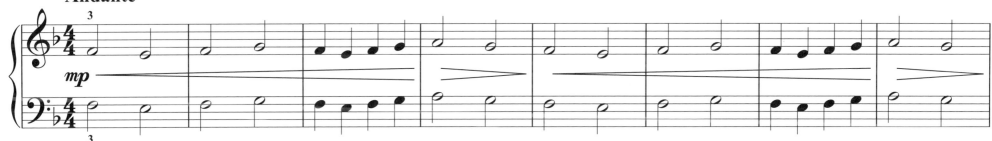
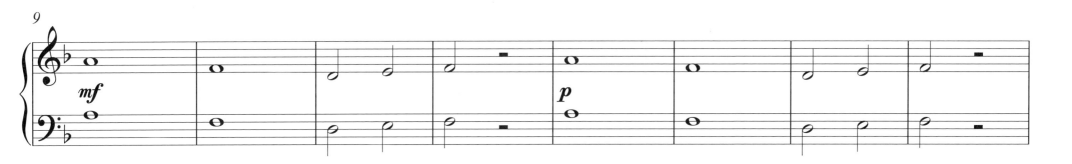

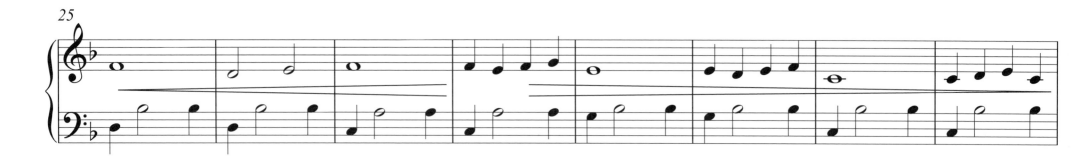

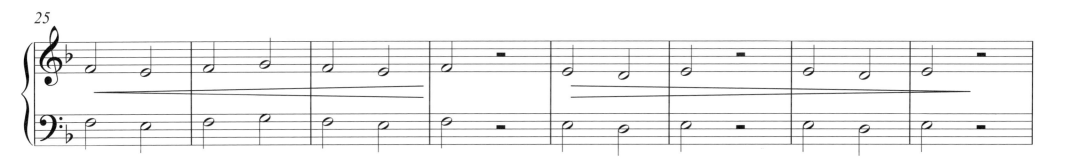

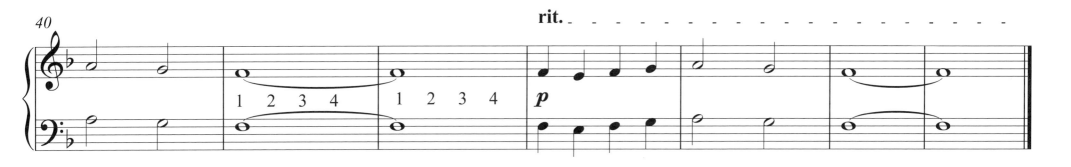

VII
Blue Note Waltz

Intermediate

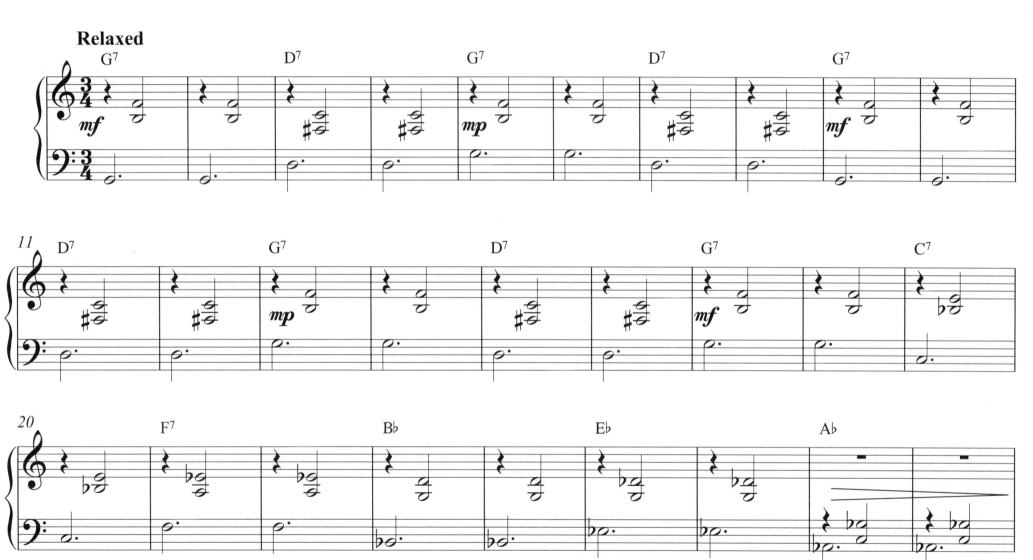

VII
Blue Note Waltz

Beginner
Both hands two octaves higher

Relaxed

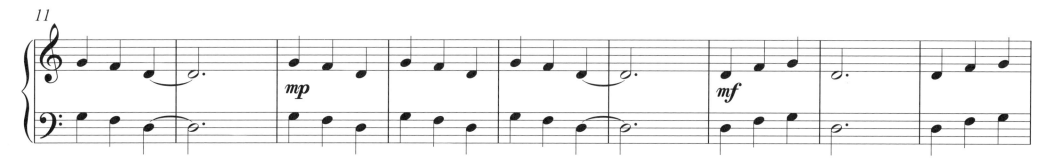
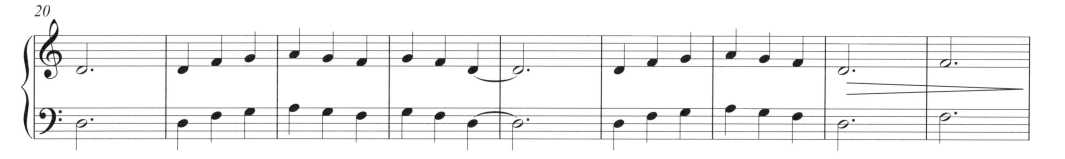

20

*Where the beginner needs to count their rests.

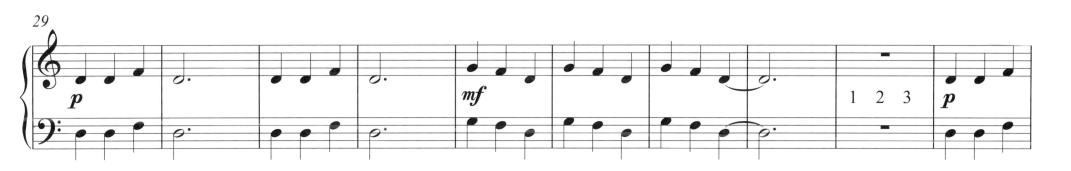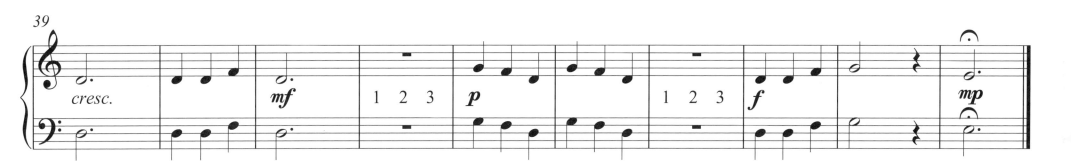

VIII
Dorian Din

VIII
Dorian Din

Beginner
Both hands one octave higher